UNDERSTANDING ARTIFICIAL INTELLIGENCE CLASS IV

DR DHEERAJ MEHROTRA

Made with ♥ on the Notion Press Platform
www.notionpress.com

Contents

Preface

Dear Young Learners,

Welcome to the fascinating world of Artificial Intelligence (AI)! This book is designed especially for you, our curious Class IV students, to help you understand AI and how it magically touches our lives daily.

Have you ever wondered how your favourite voice assistant answers your questions or how your tablet shows you cartoons you might like? That's all because of AI! Through this book, we'll take you on an exciting journey to discover the amazing things AI can do and how it helps make our lives easier, smarter, and more fun. Learning about AI will spark your imagination and inspire you to think creatively about the future. Who knows? You might grow up to invent your own AI robot or build intelligent machines to help the world!

So, let's dive into this wonderful world of Artificial Intelligence and have fun learning together. Remember, every big idea starts with a small step, and this book is your first step into the future of technology.

Happy Learning!

Author

ONE

WHAT IS ARTIFICIAL INTELLIGENCE?

What is Artificial Intelligence?

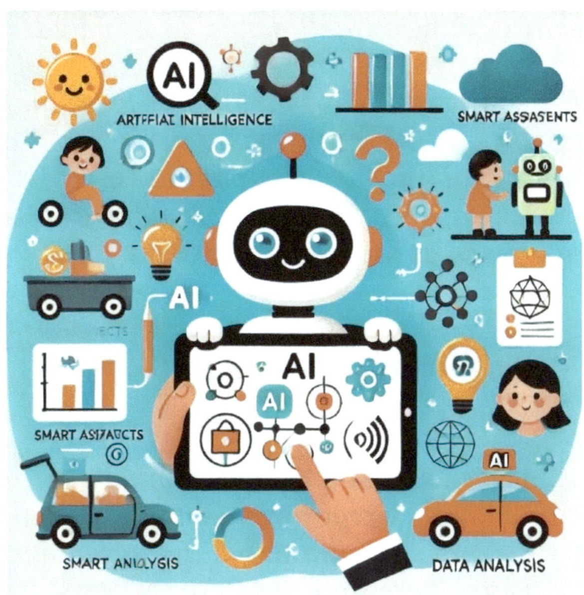

Artificial Intelligence, or AI, is like giving a brain to computers and machines so they can do clever things! Imagine if your toy robot could help you with your homework or if your family car could drive itself to school.

Artificial Intelligence, or AI, is the science of making computers and machines smart. It helps them perform tasks that usually require human thought, such as solving puzzles, recognizing faces, or talking to people.

AI doesn't think like us but learns from what we teach it. Imagine having a robot friend who can help with homework or a car that drives independently. That's AI in action!

As a branch of Computer Science:

Artificial Intelligence (AI) is a branch of computer science that aims to create machines capable of performing tasks that typically require human intelligence. This includes learning, reasoning, problem-solving, perception, language understanding, and decision-making. AI technologies are increasingly integrated into various sectors, enhancing efficiency and enabling new capabilities. This document explores the definition of AI and provides examples of its implementation across different industries.

As a Simulation of Human Intelligence (HI):

Artificial Intelligence (AI) is the simulation of human intelligence in machines programmed to think and learn like humans. AI systems can analyze data, recognize patterns, and make decisions based on the information gathered. The field of AI encompasses various subfields, including machine learning, natural language processing, robotics, and computer vision.

AI doesn't think like humans do. Instead, it learns from the information we give it. For example, if we show a computer many pictures of cats and dogs, it can learn to tell the difference between them. It's like when you learn to recognize your friends by looking at their faces!

Examples of AI in Everyday Life

1. Smart Voice Assistants

What It Is: AI-powered helpers like Siri, Alexa, and Google Assistant.

What It Does: They answer questions, play music, set alarms, and even tell jokes!

For example, ask, "What's the weather today?" or "Play my favourite song."

2. Online Learning

What It Is: AI is used in educational apps and websites.

What It Does: AI helps students with homework, explains math problems, and suggests fun learning videos.

Example: Apps like Khan Academy or Duolingo use AI to help you learn at your own pace.

3. Video Recommendations

What It Is: Platforms like YouTube and Netflix use AI.

What It Does: AI remembers the videos, shows you like, and suggests new ones you might enjoy.

Example: You watch a cartoon on YouTube, and AI recommends similar fun videos.

4. Video Games

What It Is: AI is used in games to make characters smart.

What It Does: It makes the game challenging and exciting by acting like a real opponent.

Example: AI in chess or racing games competes against you like another player.

5. Smart Cameras

What It Is: AI is built into cameras and phones.

What It Does: It helps focus on faces, removes blurriness, and even suggests a perfect photo smile.

Example: When you smile for a selfie, AI adjusts the camera settings for the best picture.

6. Navigation and Maps

What It Is: AI is used in apps like Google Maps and Waze.

What It Does: It shows the fastest route and alerts you about traffic or roadblocks.

Example: Your parents use Google Maps to find the best way to school or a park.

7. Shopping Online

What It Is: AI is used in shopping websites like Amazon.

What It Does: It suggests products you might like based on your previous purchase.

Example: If you search for toys, AI recommends more fun toys for you.

8. Robots in Real Life

What It Is: Robots use AI to do tasks.

What It Does: They can clean the floor, help in factories, or even deliver food!

Example: A robotic vacuum cleaner cleans your house while you play.

9. AI in Health

What It Is: AI helps doctors and hospitals.

What It Does: It helps doctors discover what's wrong and suggests the best treatment.

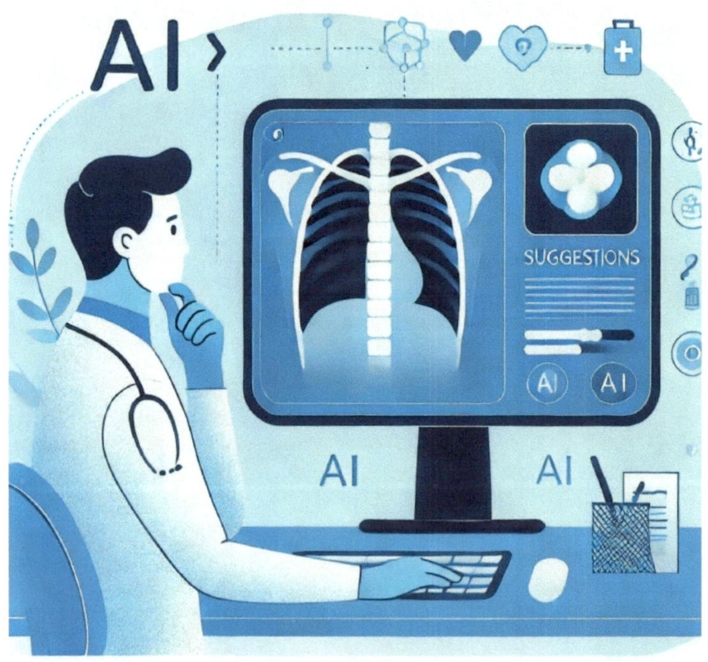

Example: AI can look at an X-ray and tell the doctor what might be wrong.

10. AI for Fun

What It Is: Apps and tools use AI for creativity.

What It Does: AI helps you draw, colour pictures, or create fun animations.

Example: Apps like AutoDraw turn your rough sketches into perfect drawings.

Questions & Answers

Question 1: What is Artificial Intelligence (AI)?
Answer: AI is the science of making computers and machines smart to perform tasks that usually require human intelligence, like solving puzzles, recognizing faces, or talking to people.

Question 2: How does AI learn?
Answer: AI learns from the information we give it, such as analyzing patterns or recognizing objects from examples.

Question 3: What is one example of AI in voice assistants?
Answer: AI in voice assistants like Alexa or Siri can answer questions, play music, and set alarms.

Question 4: Name an educational app that uses AI.
Answer: Apps like Khan Academy and Duolingo use AI to help students learn independently.

Question 5: How does AI suggest videos on platforms like YouTube?
Answer: AI remembers the videos you watch and suggests similar ones you might enjoy.

Question 6: How does AI make video games more exciting?
Answer: AI makes game characters smart, acting like real opponents to make the game challenging.

Question 7: What is an example of AI in smart cameras?
Answer: AI in cameras helps focus on faces, removes blur, and suggests the best smile for photos.

Question 8: How does AI help with navigation?
Answer: AI in apps like Google Maps shows the fastest route and alerts about traffic or roadblocks.

Question 9: How does AI personalize online shopping?
Answer: AI on websites like Amazon suggests products based on your previous searches and purchases.

Question 10: What can robots powered by AI do?
Answer: AI-powered robots can clean floors, work in factories, or deliver food.

Question 11: How does AI assist doctors in healthcare?

Answer: AI helps doctors analyze data, like X-rays, to find out what's wrong and suggest treatments.

Question 12: What is an example of AI for creativity?

Answer: Apps like AutoDraw use AI to turn rough sketches into polished drawings.

Question 13: How is AI used in video recommendations?

Answer: AI analyzes your preferences and suggests videos you might enjoy based on what you've watched.

Question 14: Why is AI helpful for students in education?

Answer: AI helps explain math problems, suggest learning materials, and customize student lessons.

Question 15: What is an example of AI in everyday navigation?

Answer: AI in Google Maps helps find the best route to school or a park.

TWO
HOW AI LEARNS?

How AI Learns?

*AI learns through a process called **machine learning**.*

Here's how it works:

***Data**: AI looks at lots of information, like pictures, sounds, or text.*

***Practice**: It tries to solve problems or answer questions using the data.*

***Improvement**: If it makes mistakes, it learns to improve next time.*

AI, or Artificial Intelligence, learns similarly to how you learn new things in school. Imagine teaching a robot to do something, like recognizing animals, playing a game, or solving a puzzle. Here's how it works step by step:

Step 1: Learning with Information (Data)

AI starts by looking at lots of information. This information can be pictures, sounds, or words.

AI starts learning by looking at lots of information, such as pictures, sounds, and words.

Example:

If you teach the robot about animals, you show it pictures of cats and dogs. The robot looks carefully and starts noticing things like, "Cats usually have pointy ears, and dogs often have floppy ears."

Step 2: Practice Makes Perfect

After learning from the pictures, the robot practices using what it learned. It tries to solve problems or answer questions based on the information.

Here is an image showing a friendly robot practicing what it has learned by solving simple puzzles, like identifying animals or answering questions.

Example:
You show the robot a new picture and ask, "Is this a cat or a dog?" The robot tries to guess using what it learned.

Step 3: Learning from Mistakes

Sometimes, the robot makes a mistake. That's okay! It learns from its mistakes and improves for the next time.

Example: If the robot calls a dog a cat, you tell it, "No, that's a dog!" The robot remembers this and gets better at recognizing dogs.

Why is AI Learning Similar to Your Learning?

You Learn from Examples: Just like your teacher shows examples to explain something, AI uses data to learn.

You Practice Problems: When you solve math problems, you get better. AI practices, too, by trying different things.

You Learn from Mistakes: If your teacher corrects your work, you will remember it for the next time. AI does the same!

Fun Example for You

Imagine you're teaching a robot to play Tic-Tac-Toe. At first, it doesn't know where to place its "X" or "O." After playing with you many times, the robot understands the best moves. Over time, it gets so good that it might even win against you! That's how AI learns—by practising and improving.

What Makes AI Learning Special?

AI can learn much faster than humans because it can process a lot of information very quickly. It helps us in extraordinary ways, such as recognizing faces, answering questions, and even helping doctors. AI is like a super-smart student who's constantly improving!

Questions & Answers

Question 1: What is the process called through which AI learns?

Answer: The process is called machine learning.

Question 2: What type of information does AI use to learn?

Answer: AI uses data like pictures, sounds, and words to learn.

Question 3: How does AI practice after learning?

Answer: AI practices by solving problems or answering questions using the learned information.

Question 4: What happens when AI makes a mistake?

Answer: When AI makes a mistake, it learns from it and improves for the next time.

Question 5: How does AI learn about animals?

Answer: AI learns about animals by looking at pictures of cats and dogs and noticing features like pointy ears for cats and floppy ears for dogs.

Question 6: How is AI's learning similar to your learning in school?

Answer: Just like you learn from examples, practice problems, and correct mistakes, AI learns similarly.

Question 7: Give an example of AI practising what it has learned.

Answer: If AI sees a new picture of an animal, it uses what it has learned to guess whether it is a cat or a dog.

Question 8: What does AI do when incorrectly identifying a dog as a cat?

Answer: AI will remember the corrections and better recognise dogs in the future.

Question 9: What is a fun example of AI learning?

Answer: Teach a robot to play Tic-Tac-Toe and watch it improve with each game.

Question 10: Why is AI called a "super-smart student"?

Answer: AI is called a "super-smart student" because it can learn quickly by processing a lot of information.

Question 11: How does AI help in extraordinary ways?

Answer: AI helps recognise faces, answer questions, and assist doctors.

Question 12: Why can AI learn faster than humans?

Answer: AI can process a large amount of information very quickly.

Question 13: What is an example of how AI learns from mistakes?

Answer: If AI calls a dog a cat, it learns from the correction and remembers it for the next time.

Question 14: How does AI understand the best moves in Tic-Tac-Toe?

Answer: By playing the game many times and learning from its mistakes.

Question 15: What does AI do with the information it looks at during the first learning step?

Answer: AI analyzes the information to notice patterns and features, like distinguishing cats from dogs.

THREE

AI Around Us

AI Around Us

AI helps us every day. Here are some examples:

Voice Assistants: Tools like Siri or Alexa answer questions and help with tasks.**Smartphones**: AI helps improve photos and predict what you're typing.**Games**: AI makes video games challenging and fun by acting like a competent opponent.**Shopping Apps**: AI suggests items you might like based on your previous purchase.**Maps**: AI shows the best routes to avoid traffic.

AI, or Artificial Intelligence, is like a magical helper working behind the scenes to make things easier and more fun. Let's look at some simple examples of how AI helps us daily!

1. Voice Assistants

What It Does: Voice assistants like Siri and Alexa are like friendly robots listening to and answering your questions.
Example: If you ask, "What's the weather today?" they can tell you if it's sunny or rainy. You can also ask them to play your favourite song or set the alarm.
Why It's Helpful: Voice assistants help us by answering questions and doing tasks.

2. Smartphones

What It Does: AI in smartphones makes your pictures look better and helps you type faster.
Example: When you take a photo, AI can adjust the colours and brightness to make it look beautiful. When you type a message, AI guesses what you want to say next.
Why It's Helpful: AI makes your photos friendly and helps you save time while typing.

3. Games

What It Does: In video games, AI acts like an intelligent opponent to make the game exciting.
Example: When you play a racing game, AI drives the other cars to compete against you, just like a real player would.
Why It's Helpful: AI makes video games more fun and challenging.

4. Shopping Apps

What It Does: AI in shopping apps suggests things you might like based on your purchase.
For example, if you buy a toy car, the app might suggest a toy garage because it thinks you'll like it, too.
Why It's Helpful: AI helps you find more items you might love.

5. Maps

What It Does: AI in maps helps us find the best way to go somewhere.
Example: If there's a traffic jam, AI will show you a different road so you can reach your destination faster.
Why It's Helpful: AI saves time by finding the quickest and easiest routes.

Questions & Answers

Question 1: What are voice assistants like Siri and Alexa used for?
Answer: Voice assistants answer questions, play music, set alarms, and assist with tasks.

Question 2: How does AI improve photos on smartphones?
Answer: AI adjusts the colours and brightness to make photos look better.

Question 3: How does AI help when you type a message on a smartphone?
Answer: AI guesses what you want to say next, making typing faster and easier.

Question 4: What does AI do in video games?
Answer: AI acts as an intelligent opponent, making the game more fun and challenging by competing like a real player.

Question 5: How does AI in shopping apps suggest items you might like?
Answer: AI analyzes your previous purchases and suggests related items you might enjoy.

Question 6: What happens when there's a traffic jam and you use a map app?

Answer: AI finds a different road and shows you the quickest way to avoid the traffic jam.

Question 7: Give an example of how a voice assistant can help you.

Answer: You can ask a voice assistant, "What's the weather today?" it will tell you if it's sunny or rainy.

Question 8: Why is AI helpful in smartphones?

Answer: AI makes photos look better and helps save time by predicting text while typing.

Question 9: Why does AI make video games more exciting?

Answer: AI makes games exciting by acting as an intelligent opponent and challenging players in a fun way.

Question 10: How does AI in maps help us save time?

Answer: AI shows the quickest and easiest routes to reach our destination.

FOUR
FUN THINGS TO DO WITH AI

Fun Things to Do with AI

Explore AI in fun ways:

Create with AI: *Use apps that turn your drawings into art.*

Talk to AI: *Ask a voice assistant to tell you jokes or stories.*

Play Games: *Challenge AI in a game like chess or tic-tac-toe.*

Try Coding: *Use simple tools like Scratch to create AI projects.*

Learning about AI Through Play

1. Create with AI

What You Can Do:

Draw a straightforward cat and watch AI make it look different

Colour pictures and see AI bring them to life

Make silly faces and let AI turn them into cartoons

Fun Activity: "My AI Art Gallery"

Draw three different animals

Use an AI art app to transform them

Show your friends how different they look!

2. Talk to AI

Fun Things to Try:

Ask, "Tell me a funny joke about animals."

Say, "What sound does a dinosaur make?"

Request "Tell me a short story about space."

Activity: "AI Friend Game"

Make a list of 5 funny questions

Ask AI and write down its answers

Share the funniest response with your class

3. Play with AI

Games to Try:

Tic-tac-toe against the computer

Simple chess games for beginners

Memory matching games

Fun Challenge: "Beat the Computer"

Play tic-tac-toe 3 times

Try different moves each time

See if you can win!

4. Simple Coding

Easy Projects:

Make a cat move across the screen

Create a simple greeting program

Design a basic number-guessing game

Short Questions and Answers

Q1: What is AI? AI is like a brilliant computer friend who can learn and help us do things.

Q2: Can AI draw pictures? A: Yes! AI can help make our drawings look different and colourful.

Q3: Do we use AI every day? A: Yes! When we ask Alexa questions or play computer games, we're using AI.

Q4: Can AI tell stories? A: Yes! AI can tell us fun stories and jokes when we ask.

Q5: Is AI smarter than humans? A: No, AI is just a helpful tool humans created to make tasks easier.

Fun Class Activity: "My AI Helper"

Draw and Answer:

Draw what you think AI looks like

Write one way AI helps you

Draw your favourite AI game

Remember:

AI is here to help us learn and have fun

Always use AI with a grown-up nearby

Share your AI creations with friends

FIVE

AI AND SAFETY

AI and Safety

AI is cool, but we must use it safely. Here's how:

Be Smart Online: Don't share your details with apps or websites.

Ask an Adult: If unsure about an AI tool, check with a parent or teacher.

Use it for Good: Use AI to learn, play, or help others, not to harm anyone.

How to Use AI Safely

AI is a fascinating tool that can help us learn and have fun, but it's essential to use it safely. Here are some easy tips for you to follow:

1. Be Smart Online

Tip: *Don't share details like your name, address, or phone number with apps or websites.*

Why it matters: *Sharing personal information can put you at risk. Always keep your information private!*

2. Ask an Adult

Tip: *Always check with a parent or teacher if unsure about an AI tool or how to use it.*

Why it matters: *Adults can help you understand whether something is safe. It's always good to ask for help!*

3. Use it for Good

Tip: *Use AI to learn new things, play games, or help others. Avoid using it to harm anyone or do bad things.*

Why it matters: *AI can be a powerful tool for good. Let's use it to make the world a better place!*

Short Answer Questions

Question 1: Why should you not share your details online?

Answer: You should not share your details online, as doing so can put you at risk.

Question 2: Who should you ask if you are unsure about using an AI tool?

Answer: If you are unsure about using an AI tool, ask an adult, such as a parent or teacher.

Question 3: What are some good ways to use AI?

Answer: You can use AI to learn new things, play games, or help others.

Question 4: Why is it important to use AI for good?

Answer: It is important to use AI for good because it can improve the world and keep everyone safe.

SIX
HOW AI HELPS THE WORLD?

How AI Helps the World

AI is used in amazing ways to help people:

In Hospitals: AI helps doctors find diseases faster.

In Schools: AI makes learning fun with apps and tools.

In Nature: AI tracks animals and protects forests.

In Space: AI helps scientists explore planets and stars.

AI transforms how we live and learn, from healthcare to education, nature conservation, and space exploration.

AI in Hospitals

In hospitals, AI is like a superhero for doctors! It helps them find diseases faster and more accurately. For example, AI can quickly review many tests and images if a doctor is trying to determine if someone has a specific illness. This means patients can get the proper treatment sooner, which helps them feel better faster!

AI in Schools

AI makes learning fun and exciting! Many apps and tools use AI to help kids learn. For instance, some games teach math or reading entertainingly. These apps can adapt to a child's performance, ensuring they are consistently challenged but not too hard. This way, learning becomes an adventure!

AI in Nature

AI is also a friend of nature! It helps scientists track animals and protect forests. For example, AI can analyze pictures taken by cameras in the wild to determine the number of animals in a particular area. This helps keep track of endangered species and ensures their safety. AI can also help monitor forests to prevent illegal logging and protect our planet.

AI in Space

In space, AI is like a trusty sidekick for scientists! It helps them explore planets and stars. For example, AI can analyze data from telescopes and spacecraft to find new planets or study the stars. This allows us to learn more about the universe and our place in it!

Other Ways AI Can Help

There are many other ways AI can help! Here are a few ideas:

• 41 •

In Homes: *AI can help us with chores, like vacuuming or managing our schedules.*

In Transportation: *AI can help make cars safer by warning drivers of dangers or even driving the car itself!*

In Entertainment: *AI can create new games or movies that we can enjoy.*

Short Answer Questions

Question: 1 How does AI help doctors in hospitals?

AI helps doctors find diseases faster by analyzing tests and images quickly.

Question: 2 What is one way AI makes learning fun in schools?

AI uses apps and games that adapt to a child's performance, making learning exciting.

Question: 3 How does AI help protect nature?

AI tracks animals and monitors forests to prevent illegal activities and protect wildlife.

Question: 4 What role does AI play in space exploration?

AI analyzes data from telescopes and spacecraft to help scientists discover new planets and study stars.

Question: 5 Can you name another area where AI can help?

AI can help in homes by managing chores or schedules, making life easier for everyone!

SEVEN
THE FUTURE OF AI

The Future of AI

AI is constantly improving. In the future, we might see:

Robots help with household chores.

AI helps farmers grow more food.

Self-driving cars on every road.

Maybe you'll even grow up to invent a new kind of AI that changes the world!

AI is a constantly improving technology; soon, we might see robots doing chores, helping farmers, and even self-driving cars on our roads. Imagine being the person who invented a new kind of AI that makes the world a better place!

Robots Helping with Household Chores

In the future, we might have robots to help us with our chores at home. These robots could clean our rooms, wash the dishes, or even cook our meals! Just think about how much time we would save if we didn't have to do these tasks ourselves. We could spend more time playing, studying, or hanging out with friends and family.

AI Helping Farmers Grow More Food

Farmers work very hard to grow the food we eat. In the future, AI could help them do this even better. For example, AI can analyze the soil and weather conditions to tell farmers the best time to plant crops. This means that farmers could grow more food and help feed everyone worldwide. With AI, we could have healthier and more delicious food!

Self-Driving Cars on Every Road

Imagine getting into a car that drives itself! In the future, we might have self-driving cars on every road. These cars would use AI to understand the traffic, follow the rules, and take us wherever we want. This would make travelling safer and more manageable, and we could relax or do other things while the car drives us.

You Could Invent a New Kind of AI!

Who knows? Maybe one day, you will grow up to invent a new kind of AI that changes the world! You could create *something that helps people, makes life easier, or even solves big problems like climate change. The possibilities are endless, and the future is bright for those who dream big!*

By understanding these exciting possibilities, we can look forward to a future where AI plays a significant role in our lives!

Short Answer Questions

1. What tasks might robots help us with in the future?

Robots might help us with cleaning, washing dishes, and cooking meals.

2. How can AI help farmers?

AI can analyze soil and weather conditions to help farmers know the best time to plant crops, allowing them to grow more food.

3. What is a self-driving car?

A self-driving car is a vehicle that uses AI to drive itself without needing a human to control it.

4. What could you do in the future related to AI?

Glossary:

Artificial Intelligence (AI): Making computers and machines bright.

Machine Learning: A way AI learns by practising with data.

Data: Information like pictures, numbers, or sounds.

Voice Assistant: An innovative tool that talks to you and answers questions.

Activity Page:

Invent Your AI Helper: Draw a picture of your desired AI robot. What will it do?

Find AI Around You: Look around your house or school. Write down three ways AI is helping you.

Ask AI a Question: Use a voice assistant to ask something interesting. Write down the answer.

EIGHT
Ethical Use of AI

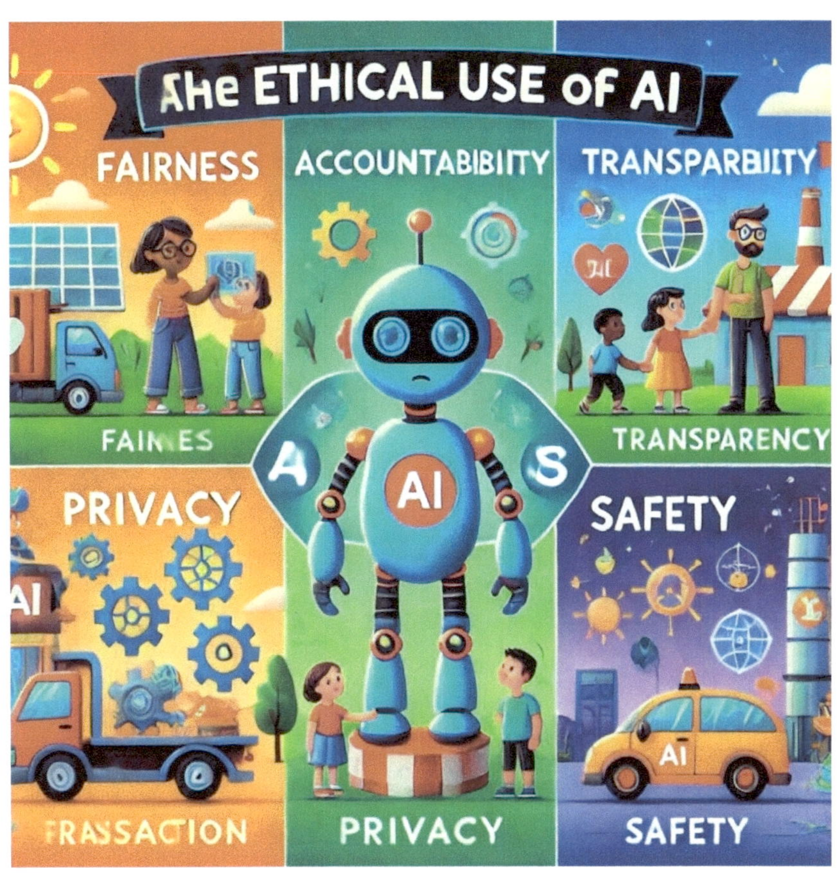

AI, or Artificial Intelligence, is like a super-smart robot or computer program that helps us in many ways. But to ensure AI is helpful and safe for everyone, we must follow some essential rules. Let's look at these rules.

1. Fairness

What It Means:
AI must treat everyone equally, no matter who they are.
Example:
Imagine a robot teacher giving everyone the same chance to answer questions, regardless of where they come from or how they look. That's fairness!
Why It's Important:
Fairness ensures that AI helps everyone equally without being unfair or biased.

2. Accountability

What It Means:
People who create and use AI must take responsibility for how it works.
Example:
If an AI app gives the wrong answer, the developers should fix it and explain what happened.
Why It's Important:
Being responsible builds trust and ensures AI works correctly.

3. Transparency

What It Means:
We should be able to understand how AI works and what it does.
Example:
If an intelligent assistant suggests a song, it should explain, "I picked this because it's similar to the songs you like."
Why It's Important:
Transparency helps us trust AI because we know how it makes decisions.

4. Privacy

What It Means:
AI must protect our personal information, like our name or address.
Example:
When you use an AI-powered app, it should keep your information safe and not share it with others without permission.
Why It's Important:
Protecting privacy ensures everyone feels safe using AI.

5. Safety and Security

What It Means:
AI should be designed to keep everyone safe and not cause harm.
Example:
A self-driving car must be tested to ensure it drives safely and doesn't get into accidents.
Why It's Important:
Safety is essential so AI can be trusted to help us without causing problems.

Why Are These Rules Important?

These rules help us use AI in ways that benefit everyone. They ensure that AI is fair, safe, and trustworthy. If we follow these rules, AI can improve our lives without harming us.

AI is like a super-smart helper, but we must ensure it follows rules to treat everyone fairly, protect privacy, and keep us safe. By learning and following these rules, we can use AI responsibly to create a better world for everyone!

Solved Short Answer Questions

Question 1: What does fairness in AI mean?

Answer: Fairness in AI means that AI must treat everyone equally, no matter who they are.

Question 2: Why is fairness essential in AI?

Answer: Fairness ensures that AI helps everyone equally without being unfair or biased.

Question 3: What does accountability in AI mean?

Answer: Accountability means that people who create and use AI must take responsibility for how it works.

Question 4: Give an example of accountability in AI.

Answer: If an AI app gives the wrong answer, the developers should fix it and explain what happened.

Question 5: What does transparency in AI mean?

Answer: Transparency means we should be able to understand how AI works and what it does.

Question 6: Why is transparency important in AI?

Answer: Transparency helps us trust AI because we know how it makes decisions.

Question 7: How should AI protect our privacy?

Answer: AI must protect personal information, such as names and addresses, and not share it without permission.

Question 8: Give an example of how AI ensures safety and security.

Answer: A self-driving car must be tested to ensure it drives safely and avoids accidents.

Question 9: Why are rules like fairness, accountability, and safety important for AI?

Answer: These rules ensure that AI is fair, safe, and trustworthy, benefiting everyone without causing harm.

Question 10: How can following ethical rules in AI create a better world?

Answer: Following ethical rules ensures that AI treats everyone fairly, protects privacy, keeps people safe, and improves lives responsibly.

About The Author

Dheeraj Mehrotra, a white and a yellow belt in SIX SIGMA, a Certified NLP Business Diploma holder, is an Educational Innovator, Author with expertise in Six Sigma In Education, Academic Audits, Neuro-Linguistic Programming (NLP), Total Quality Management In Education, an Experiential Educator, a CBSE Resource towards School Assessment (SQAA), CCE, JIT, Five S, and KAIZEN. He has authored over 100 books on computer science, AI, digital body language, NLP, quality circles, school management, classroom effectiveness, and safety and security. A former Principal at De Indian Public School, New Delhi, (INDIA), NPS International School, Guwahati, Kunwar's Global School, Lucknow and an Education Officer at GEMS, Gurgaon, with ample teaching experience of over Three Decades, he is a certified Trainer for Quality Circles/ TQM in Education and QCI Standards for School Accreditation/ School Audits and Management. He has also been honoured with the President of India's National Teacher Award in 2006 and the Best Science Teacher State Award (By the Ministry of Science and Technology, State of UP), among others. He has published over 100 books and developed 150 FREE EDUCATIONAL MOBILE Apps for the Google Play Store exclusively for Teachers, Students, and Parents. This work has been recognised by the LIMCA BOOK OF RECORDS and INDIA BOOK OF RECORDS as the only Indian to draw that feast. As a premium UDEMY Instructor, he has developed over 500 courses and caters to over 8 Lakh students from 180 countries. As a founder and president of the IoT Society of India, he also promotes Technology Globally. Dr Mehrotra is presently engaged as a REGIONAL HEAD of the GEMS EDUCATION India Region.

Books By The Same Author

Scan Here To Know More